Cats

# Burmilla Cats

Launch!
An Imprint of Abdo Zoom
abdobooks.com

Leo Statts

abdobooks.com

Published by Abdo Zoom, a division of ABDO, PO Box 398166, Minneapolis, Minnesota 55439.

Launch!™ is a trademark and logo of Abdo Zoom.

Printed in the United States of America, North Mankato, Minnesota.

052019
092019

THIS BOOK CONTAINS RECYCLED MATERIALS

Photo Credits: iStock, Shutterstock

Production Contributors: Kenny Abdo, Jennie Forsberg, Grace Hansen, John Hansen

Design Contributors: Dorothy Toth, Neil Klinepier

Library of Congress Control Number: 2018963136

Publisher's Cataloging-in-Publication Data

Names: Statts, Leo, author.

Title: Burmilla cats / by Leo Statts.

Description: Minneapolis, Minnesota : Abdo Zoom, 2020 | Series: Cats | Includes online resources and index.

Identifiers: ISBN 9781532127090 (lib. bdg.) | ISBN 9781532128073 (ebook) | ISBN 9781532128561 (Read-to-me ebook)

Subjects: LCSH: Burmilla cat--Juvenile literature. | Cat, Domestic--Juvenile literature. | Cats--Behavior--Juvenile literature. | Cat breeds--Juvenile literature.

Classification: DDC 636.8--dc23

# Table of Contents

# Burmilla Cats

Burmilla Cats are known for their pretty fur **coats**. Their coats can appear to sparkle!

# Body

Burmilla cats can be longhaired or shorthaired.

Longhairs will have **tufts** in their ears. They also have fluffy tails.

Burmilla cats have round heads. They have large ears. Their eyes are also big. The eyes are often a **shade** of green.

Burmilla cats have short, little legs. Their paws are oval in shape.

# Care

Burmilla cats need to be brushed weekly. Brushing removes dead hair.

Their teeth should also be brushed.

Burmilla Cats also often need their ears cleaned and their nails trimmed.

They like their litter boxes to be kept very clean.

# Personality

Burmilla cats are gentle and loving. They enjoy attention from their families.

These cats are also smart. They love learning new tricks and playing with toys.

# History

Burmilla cats were first bred in England. They are a mix of Burmese and Persian cats. Burmilla cats have been around since the 1980s.

Quick Stats

# Average Weight

**A male Burmilla cat weighs less than a bowling ball.**

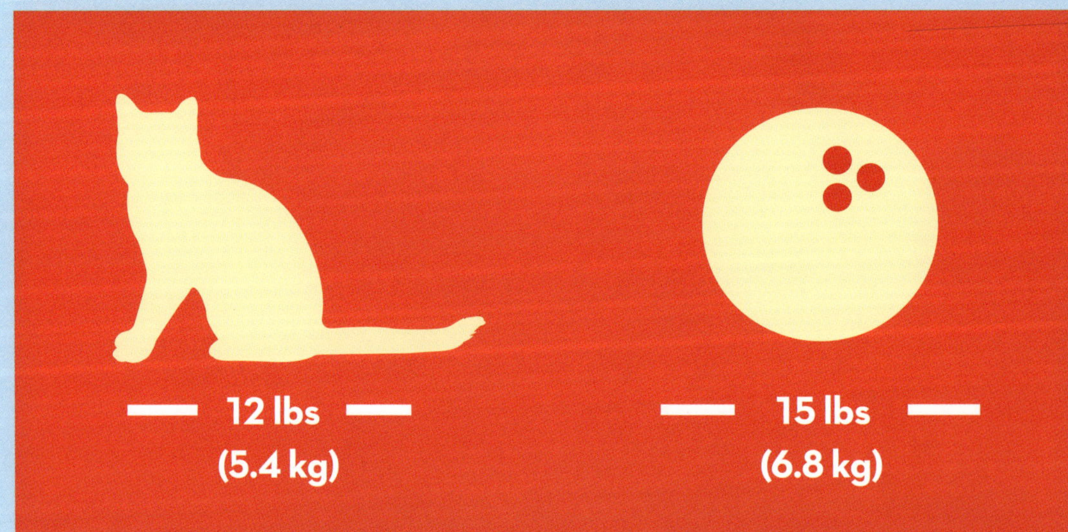

Quick Stats

# Average Height

## A female Burmilla cat is taller than a basketball.

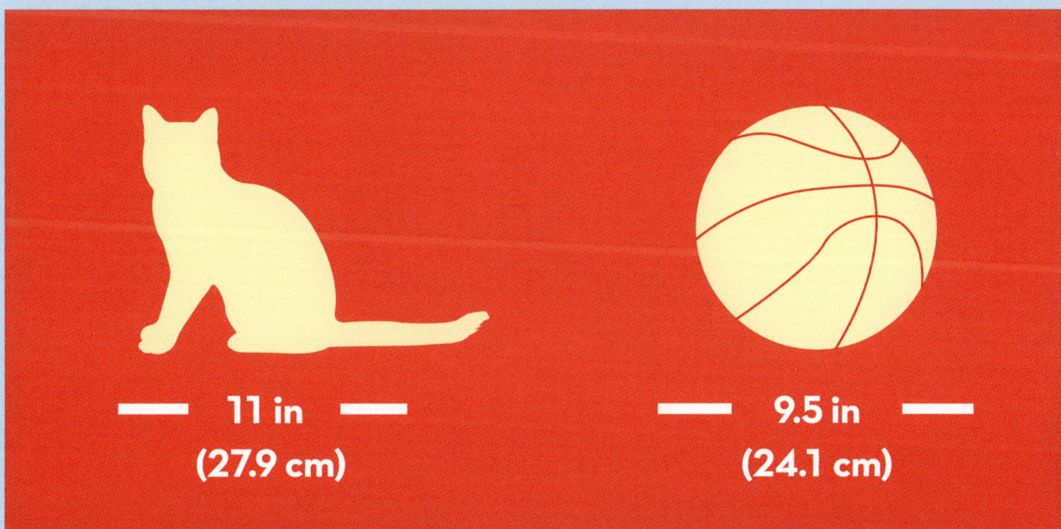

# Glossary

**bred** – made to look a certain way.

**coat** – the hair that covers an animal's body.

**shade** – how light or dark a color is.

**tufts** – a bunch of hair growing together in the same place.

# Online Resources

Booklinks
NONFICTION NETWORK
FREE! ONLINE NONFICTION RESOURCES

For more information on Burmilla cats, please visit **abdobooklinks.com** or scan this QR code.

---

Abdo Zoom
DATABASES
BEGINNING ONLINE RESEARCH

Learn even more with the Abdo Zoom Animals database. Visit **abdozoom.com** today!

# Index